THE
SPIRIT
OF
POETRY

In The Spirit of Poetry

JD VANANDEN

THE SPIRIT OF POETRY
IN THE SPIRIT OF POETRY

iUniverse books may be ordered through booksellers or by contacting:

iUniverse
1663 Liberty Drive
Bloomington, IN 47403
www.iuniverse.com
844-349-9409

ISBN: 978-1-6632-3403-2 (sc)
ISBN: 978-1-6632-3402-5 (e)

Print information available on the last page.

iUniverse rev. date: 12/23/2021

10

Thru, the past,
Our keen sense,
Relives, until the future sense.
A memory, ones unique existence,
A vital role. For lessons of the heart,
Replace one, for the living of their time.
A memory lives on.
One from You and Here is mine.
This is my time,
Soon, within the futures outlook.
A memory of my own,
I will leave behind.

9/26/2012

Time has passed,
since your departure,
from this relentless, " World"
No one, has made me,
feel, such as you did.
In my Heart, always.
Within, my thoughts... Even Now.
I will always, Love You...
I will, Miss You dearly..,
How I wish.. How I wish...
(You were and still are, My Distant from A Far)

A lengthy commitment,

Abide to these un relentless tides

Of change the conformities of life are desired no more.

The solitude of stipulation confronts a builder of much more.

Such a foundation, that can withstand these falls.

The pain of infliction.

Withstanding no more,

Gasp once, twice for the

Luring existence of one more.

The presence of The Almighty, leads on.

The future is now, shall we abide,

Or just move on.

Conquer all.

Which falls. Upon you.

Adequately Beautiful

At a quick glimpse
It all seems un real.
A possible hint,
Left for all, the un seen.

The grass rolls and tumbles
As a light cross wind,
Creates any sort of movement.
Spotty colors of red and orange
Change the vast visual, within view.

A narrow trail meanders until you see
Two fruitful tress
Adjacent but alone from
Any other deciduous life.
Leaves rustle amongst the breeze,
As once ripe fruit slowly decays..

In the vast distance, mountains
Roll with autumns impetuous signs.
Above, the sky is blue. The sounds of
Birds chirping echoes for a slight instant.

As the wind decides which way to go
Yellow petal flowers sway and bounce,
As the field is full, as pollinators attempt to land. Most are
left vigorously at a return approach.

Many trees are left swaying,
While their leaves from the crown.
Loose their abscission layer.
Only to be blown away.

Over head, the horizon steadily
Falls as the breath
From the beauty settles in,
For the evening hour.
Sets the journey homeward.

Turning back a final time.
The Autumn colors,
Help beautify, this portrait
From any other seasonal change.

Adhere to the fixations,

That brought you here.

Never conform to societies,

Way's or permanent thoughts.

Listen to everything, believe nothing.

You give everything to receive nothing.

You want love, only to get rejection.

Real pain, is that, in which nobody sees.

Beauty, is so much like a Rose.

Pick one and see.

How much you learn during your lifetime.

How much you see and little you do..

All at Once

Everything seemed prevalent,
It all had relevance, seemingly enough.
Occurring, as a mere endless thought.
Perpetuating, as rigorous daunting reminder.
Hopelessly, angered by the reoccurring thought.
As to ponder, a realization,
Overwhelming, tiresome as more time eludes
The obvious outcome.
Banded to reinforce the continuous dilemma.
Becoming more intolerable, as memeries fade.
My palpating heart forgives and receives endless emotional
out bursts.
For Life is
All that you
Put into it.
It Will happen to you,

All at Once.

All that follows,
Seemingly, something,
Is surely to appear.
When in the end,
There surely had to,
Be a beginning.
So when in mind,
Take the time,
Control your mind.
Abruptly, when in the end,
The beginning is all,
That now.
A Memory.
Something surely else,
Will follow.
Appear, begin,
Make new.
All over again.
Certain reasons,

I don't know why?
The memory is just
That now.
All that follows:
All that is,
Certain remains.

Alone

As I glance amongst the stars
Within the billion of galaxies
How could we walk alone
Thru already an abundance of life
Absent are the forms of beings
We may shun or deplore.
As our knowledge, explores, a vast
Array of speculation detest. A Life
greater that of our own.
Alone, we sometimes feel or deny.

Atomosphere

Although its been,

Nearly a solar year.

Your Eye's, Your Smile.

Seem to never disappear.

From Our Hearts From Our Minds.

Until it decorates

Every particle in the Thermosphere.

As the Aurora Borealis and the Aurora Australis embellish,the

Atmosphere.

As a twinkle a mist,

The darkened sky.

Your Heart awakens

As you wait for it,

To reappear.

Between Nature and Life

Inquire, guidance, question?
The Story, in which
Constantly changes.
For the Love of Life.
Instructs to obtain………
For the Love of Nature.
Our mind's eye create the hue,
To conform the horizon,
Continuous blue.
Between Nature and Life
A balance,
In which to explore…..
As the individual Story
Within nature,
Has yet to be..
Foretold…

Clearly I know

What pushes me,

What motivates me,

What brings me down?

I tend to allow more then others.

To push me, to rush me around.

I stand up to fall down.

I smile, to cheer me up.

I'll frown, only to stand up,

brush myself off.

I am, what moves me,

Keeps me strong.

I am who I am.

One day at a time.

Some days better then others.

Just trying to stay strong.

Cradle these things,

all that you have left,

place them as close as you can.

Disencumber that, of what you have lost.

Forget-me- not.

Nor shall I never,

Forget you.

Without you,

I see your presence as of,

One of a kind,

Like you, like me.

Just like all the people that we see.

How different we all can be.

How painful, sometimes it may feel,

you are there and

How I wish, to be embraced by you.

Even though it seems tough

because your grasp is so far away,

mine is here for the embrace.

Yours is felt from the distance.

No mater how far.

So it seems.

So it ends up to be.

Curl beside the
Pain and Shiver
Whence the Grief
Sorrow has no beliefs.
Many Shallow Wounds
Induce the Same Pain
Clench for Biting
Will bear Down on You
Tremble, Fear, Lash Out.
Upon your exsistance.
Crashing you to the floor.
Begging, " Please No More"
Cleanse the sores restore my Valor.

Deducible

Deriving solely on purpose
Perhaps dis concerning,
within another's,
speculating mis conception.
Replenishes, your only worries.
A vulnerable cry,
is left un spoken.
One Heart, beats as many.
This perhaps alone,
could carry you thru.

Disclosure

Frails in Comparison
Discomfort
Weakens you with age.
Dissatisfaction
Is compared only too sin.
Discouragement
Envies all that is
Saintly.
All is too much
Forgotten
Within the years
Of a Unique Life Time.
In Comparison, too
All that you already
Have now.
Life..

Embrace the Odds

Certainty is a question
That seems possible at times.

Question marks linger
Enrich the mind.

Embrace the Odds,
Because the chances are,

Highly unlikely again.
Rarity is a solemn.

Certainty questioned,
Against the odds.

From the Beginning.
Until the Farewell.

Embrace the Odds.
For, certainty is best described.

As of glimpse of Hope,
Ready to" Pass By."

For the Moment.

The Heavens The Stars

Are gazed upon.

Picturesque thru time.

Observant, such as life.

As time is portrayed in a Polaroid

For a memory, mollified for a life time.

Ridiculed from age progression.

Meant, as a keep sake.

For the Moment.

We may egress from those

Images, that remain life like.

The past gone from life now.

Lived as a memory portaled within time.

As Life continues on.

For the Moment.

Picturesque thru time..

Forward the Word.

Amongst the World.

Of his Birth of his Passion.

For Life, for all Creation .

Rejoice, give Praise.

For one life taken

Saved so many..

Even til this day.

Jesus Christ life

Should be told. Truly..

As a once lived life,

Whom footsteps we

Should, all follow.

Through times of sorts

Gather around not for today,

For a time in the present, a time of meaning,

An understanding of the faith, of all kinds.

A gathering to re marvel, a time long since, withstood, never to be have adorned.

Foretold, is the meaning a devastation,

A whim of perseverance, settles for almost better than nothing.

A single impression leaves more of what,

Is Imaginable.

Gracious Gratitude

Gracious

As sent from Heaven above

Too help others, some in dire need.

As a Gift, for every tiresome day your kindness awaits.

Your hand will always seemingly be reaching out

To aid and figure out. The particular situation at hand.

Your time and willingness too help others,

May seemed un noticed from times.

From within your heart you continue on.

Gratitude

I am thankful, appreciative,

For all your thoughtfulness.

Going beyond, the interruption.

Acknowledging, the intrusion.

With thoughtfulness, the propriety

Of your heart, shall never respite.

From the Inner Grace,

Your Willingness to help others.

Truly, I am thankful

For all You do.

A Guessable Answer

The lessons are to well planned.
Criteria, motives candle their way around.
Minutes, seemed by days, per moments,
Purified with time.
Long ago, passed on certainty through the
Unfolding. Explanatory circumstance, a
Questionable beginning. Heightened, to fulfill
The unknown. Sometimes, a guessable
Answer as the very test. The sheer quaintly,
Re arranged a Hubble glance. The doubtable
We must know.
Questions put with answers.
A quotation makes it fancy.
Complete, but not entirely final.
The faint, merely pressing forward.
A capsule of time.
We are ready for our own.

H. Trae

All through the seam,
Pulls a part.
The stich,
Becomes a strand
Tediously, the seam,
Avoids the obvious.
The strong hold,
A comfort zone.
A joining together,
To take control.
The strains of this,
The pulls from that.
Only to loosen up,
Give away.
To the first one,
That gives up,
Until it's severed,
From its whole.

Helt

Great!!! A Day.

A Day Like no other.

Most are similar.

Some last forever

This one.soon

To be that.

Like no other.

A saddened frown

From today's lunacy.

Gavel my mind..

An understandable reasoning,

Who would know?

I can never Helt

Fathom such as today was.

Her Glittering Eyes

Refresh the
Once forgotten smile.
Her pace is at ease,
With herself.
With her shoulders back
And her mind at ease,
She strides forward.
Her hair so her, so beautiful.
Reminds me of, places me, a distance
From a far.
Just wondering if she too
Thinks of me. For perhaps,
There will be just one.
A refreshing smile on
Her soon, to forget my face.
That's fine which ever the case.
I have this in mind
And my very own,
Self portrait of her.
Which will be kept
Here, close at heart,
And a thank you
Close at hand.

How Your Smile
will Bring Beauty

How a smile shows,
Sincerity, elegance,
A pondering thought,
At one's first glance.

A beauty only that
You may share,
One can only hope,
This smile, reaches
Across the world.

Turning around, that
Up side down frown.
From one face to many,.
As rose like beauty.
From your precious face,
Too many, smiles you
Will bring.

Your smile brings,
Heart felt impressions,
A lasting, gesture,
A simple, beautiful,
Memorable Smile.

From one Face to many,
How Your Smile will Bring
Beauty.

Dedicated to A Beautiful Smile..

I took a bite of the un certain.

What a delight.

The taste seemed endless. I wanted more.

A sweet life, more at ease.

A tasteful treat, meaning delight.

It always pleased me and some more.

To much to little, I always wanted more.

A certain kind, for sure.

Something to live for.

Always to adore,

For sure.

I must take another bite

To be sure.

I Try Not to...

Reminisce

In past worldly tragic events.

Ponder to long

On the day eventualities.

Become saddened by loss of life. Mine too.

I Try Not to

Remember

Those loved, gone now.

Celebratious, loving expressions.

Hearing, I Love You.

Seeing, the love in your eyes.

All those years gone by.

I Try Not to

Ponder or become saddened.

Remembering, all that has been lost,

From within my heart.

I Try Not to

Even though the memories,

Fulfill my heart. Are expressed

With tears.

The years add up.
How I try not too,
Ponder to long.
My heart remembers,
What my mind can not feel.

In the foreshadows,

Behind the outlines,

Of shadows.

Traces of Hollow,

Images, signs before.

Sudden fright, wisps through,

The Hollow shadows.

Forbidden fright, lures in the night.

A rush from your heart,

Felt to your fingers.

Delivering seldom rest.

Just a stare from within the outlines.

Shadows, move about,

The stare is still there.

Fright, bestows amongst its self.

To turn on you, to feed from you,

To take you from your best.

Insanely Beautiful

We are drawn
By the mere
Gesture of your smile.
Heart felt, amongst
The pictures of countless
Arrays of glee.

Beautiful You Are,
As the pictures of you change.
From smile to smile.
From year to year.

As times moves forward.
The way, " You "
Choose to be loved,
Stays the same.

Your Smile, is the beauty,
Your Heart portrays.
Insanely Beautiful
You Are

Just need a moment,
To close my eyes,
To think for awhile,
To listen to myself.
To ponder about things,
Look around at things,
My time, alone
Away from it all.
Just for awhile
Could silence,
Be still the air.
Just for a moment
Could it all, just all
Go away,
Just for a moment
Just need a moment
To myself.

Later on, In Life.

It will teach you,

A great many things.

Sometimes, we tend

Too forget too remind,

Ourselves, to Live before

We perish. A reality we take

For granted, before it's too late.

Don't wait, live until your hearts content.

The saddest part of Living is,

Knowing, you and all your loved ones,

Share a similar but unexpected fate.

A lifetime of memories, unfortunately that's all they are..To

you.. A Hearts Expression the same as the Minds Confession.

Learn to accept

A greater loss

Learn to appreciate

At all cost

A personal gain

With standing it all

Regardless of the pain.

Forgiving The spiraling down fall.

Accepting the blame.

It all eventually converts into shame.

Building you backup

From the bottom to top.

Understanding and forgiving

You should never be ashamed.

Live to Learn

Learn to Live

A greater expectation

Is always expected

Life can seem some what
like a frown.
When everything in Your Life,
Is turned all around.
From this to all
of that.
So when in Times
of Great Happiness
In Times of Such Grief
and Sorrow.
Place your heart
and mind
aside
Just take a moment
look back
Just be who
You really are.
Kind, loving
the vast array of unique qualities.
That's who you are.

Life Itself

We may implore for more.

Criticize the humdrum

Of everyday" life."

Reluctantly, forget to give,

Thanks and Glorify thy name.

We forget to sit back

Realize the vast real picture.

The uniqueness of Life.

Within all aspects.

We live to survive.

Survive to live.

A Greater Purpose

Then our own.

Life Itself

Is best Alive.

Make the Most

Of Life.

While Your Alive

Life Itself

We may implore for more,
Try to understand futher
Never ready for the unexplainable
Try as we may
For what's in the middle.
Has little comparison from the
Beginning until the End.
Too seek out the answers
Too age old questions..
Shimmers of grace
Reflect apon our eyes..
Wishing and Wanting
Within our Hearts,
Leaning forward
Too further onward,
Life Itself

Love with your Heart,

Not your mind.

Love with your all,

For it's one of a kind.

Love is comfort that blankets you,

On all sides.

Love has to be a blessing not a disguise.

Love is an emotion in which

Your not afraid to cry,

Through times of all sorts.

Love is an everlasting impression,

Ready and stows their meaning to you.

Love is important to all of us.

Love is a gift,a present that one can share,

The meaning of life, from God.

Love is pleasure and pain,

Worth it all, just the same.

Many Images,

There may be of you.

Portrayed as others, may see.

One of you, stands tall, above

All the rest.

As many look past, a particular one.

One remains, a constant reminder.

Of how One's Life should be.

Diligent, during your course of

Life's Role.

You will always be a figure

In My Life, I shall always look

Up too.

Within, my daily life.

Within my inner thoughts.

You thought of others before yourself.

You would go without

So others wouldn't have to sacrifice.

Miss Those Days

When the time was,
Free willing
The day seemed to last,
Longer then those
Days as we aged.

The exchanging of gifts,
The Prayer before the Christmas meal.
The Love and Care
From all the memories
Handed down.

A card, wishing you well.
Bringing you joy and cheer.
For this occasion that's only
Celebrated once a year.

The daily reminder,
Of love and care.
Expressed as words of endearment.
Sometimes just I Love You,
Is all you really want to hear.

Miss Those Days

When every day seemed,
Like it would never end.
Time, dragged on.
There was time, plenty of time then.

Miss Those Days

When Life,
Had no end,
In time.

Moments Ago...

Represent yesterday's thought's
Worthwhile, for a time today.
Most are spent, relentlessly sorting them out.
Figuring, forgetting may seem overwhelming.
As the past days pile up. Too years.

Moments Ago.
Contain memories, of today's
Past experience.
Perhaps remembered later.
Or as told as a story from today.
We live life day by day.
As the days progress
Until are next birthday.

Moments Ago.
Remain the past however
The day turned out to be.

Oh Joy!!!

How thee is She?

When in need.

There must be..

A heart abundant

Like yours.

Expression, of exhilaration.

Atone, shall fill our heart.

Oh Joy!!

How thy kindred spirit,

Vows to be with one heart.

Thee seperation shall

Seem, endless, never be filled..

Compassion alone Oh Joy!!

Whose heart you shall ever free?

On Mute or Severed Mutations

Hearken, to the time that draws,

Steadies near.

The glistening pant, a reminder still.

The glowing ember, faintly moved over head.

The pale blue breath, from the crisp ripe air.

Mends the beads of eternal life.

The Hollowed sound from far beyond,

Remains a sordid to the terror stricken hull.

The paring sounds of torpid lacerations

From the duce of peine forte et dure..

One has forgotten

Their determination
A drive that
Brings fourth more
Then the dream
Can allow
One has forgotten
Their true identity.
A positive existence.
A motivation that rallies
Behind pure will.
One has forgotten
Who to be.
By J.D VanAnden..

One More Time

The sound from
The echoes distinguish
Themselves from all the rest.
A part from it all, the silence
Stirs the emotions once again.
The pain from relief
Gives hope, to surrender the
Burden from any disbelief.
One More Time
The relentless pain
For understanding, for survival,
Sets the ride in motion,
Once again. To bargain,
To familiarize just to understand.
One More Time
Only to think one
Final time.
What is there left
Inside of me?

Ordinary Life

A whispering eye
Told the story.
Growing old is very lonely.
An Ordinary Life
Thru ones precious time,
Lived a vast array of speculation.
Collective treasures,
Binded away, sunken love
Forms a shadow.
Ordinary Life
Rolls on still.
Without the rest,
Soon to love alone.
With the final day looming,
Apparent to us all.
An Ordinary Life
May rest be it still,
The best of it, portrayed away.
A plundering reminder,
Just for another day.
How it has taught too
The ones soon after.

Odoriferous

Flowers arranged
In such an odor,
A rainbow of colored flowers,
A scent to have you,
Such an aroma,
Delicate, an Image
For a perfect thought.
For a flowers beauty
Is set, in the
Beholders eyes.
A touch of elegance or maybe, surely.
Just one bouquet
Distinctively Smelling.

Patience wares you
aloofness precedes you
adjacent to the remorse
beside you lay nothing.
A figure, re taunts the
on going madness.
That is only left to remain,
an object of great detain.

Blest, who escapes
shadows inch behind you,
far beyond the dimmest light
a haunt waits for you
procceding you further
into the night

A laughing cry
swallows you
bringing you at ease.
A show of relinquished regrets
lightens the forgetting way..
By J.D Van Anden

People Are The Way

They Are Why??
Sometimes People fall
Short of being complete individuals
Step Up
We all expect certain
Things in life/out of life.
Compassion, Love and Forgiveness.
Some people choose
The selfish way.
Thanks for falling short.
Rise Up
Expectations should
Come natural.
A Shameless Flaw
Dishonestness, lack of self
Worth of ALL.
Under Appreciating,
Life's Worth For All.
Only Your thoughts and worth
Matter too You.
There is Greater Picture

For all too see.
When Your Heart
Should over whelm
Your Mind,With this
Chance,You will never.
Get it again.
Any Excuse
Will never do.

Practice the positive
Ways of living your life.
Encourage the inner being,
To in lift the mind.
To stay on the healthier side.
Discouragement, will surface
From time to time.
Welcome the positive side,
To stay near by.
Without question,
Dwell on the positive side for a change,
Already knowing.
That's the better side.
Focus on the welcome that nears,
To push along, within due time.

Reverse an exchange

Abrupt as a guest proclaims,

The innocence of the tone.

For one is left, that's all that remains.

One is left all alone.

To stand above, too look

Beyond one's range.

Pursuit of the truth.

Highly sought out, almost strange.

For told is the Greatest Book.

Your heart alone holds the proof.

Shoved behind a lonely,

Desire, kept away from a

Loving sensation. Placed,

Next to an un wanted emotion.

Hidden from your own,

God fearing image of me.

Shown relentless loving conditions.

Only, to be kept from within your care.

A love, you may be afraid to share.

Emotion less I could have never dared.

Pulled apart to love me or not.

As fragile as pedals decay.

Shoved behind a lonely,

Expiration, eventually,

It was never meant for

Ones own expending.

Disregarded, from a fear

Of your own understanding.

Assumptions, lead to greater

Misunderstandings.

Only to add more, convient speculations.
To a concern you have no interest for..
Shoved behind a lonely
Shows less for the hidden
Purpose, you or I could never deplore.

Softly, the kindness enjoyced
Amidst the waves of reluctance.
Across the the waters edge,
A beam of hope, softens the weariness
Stoic, until the feature ends.
Stern, too firm to take this Bow.
As Peace readies too fall.. Once again..
A chaotic outburst starboard side.
The Earth's fury un leashed at day twelve.
Peeks one's interest, as calmer days linger.
Always foreboding, the edge is always lingering near. Til the
peace settles, waveless.
Once Again.

Some Sort of...

Life in this Time
Expressed as Words
Meant as feelings.
From deep within the heart.
Exceptions and Conscious of Endurance.
Factor for most of this Life..

Some Sort of....

Patience's in this Time.
As a mere year
Re taunts Life
In the later years.
As the day dawns near..

Some Sort of...

Memory in this Time
When all there is left.
Is everything to decipher from.
In which that has
Not come to fruition. At this time.

Some Sort of…

Love in this Time.
When it hurts, trying
As love continues on,
Regardless of whose feelings.

Some Sort of…

Life in this Time.
Bigger then our minds
Could ever confide.
Unique in Life
As no other.
You or Me
Uniquely One of Kind.

Thankfully,

I am blessed.

With what I have.

Peacefully,

My heart

Such a subtle place

for me.

Blessed,

For truly

so is life.

Promised,

For I must

Do my part first.

Remembering,

All that I have

All that was given to me.

Pondering,

The next few steps.

Forward, within the footprints.

Loving,

In his memory

From my own heart.
Caring, so are you, Blessed.
There is no in difference's.
Sharing,
All that I have
With appreciation and
Much Thanksgiving.
By J.D VanAnden

The Expressions of Me

Picture me,

As you want,

As you can.

Your free will.

Look apon me,

Just to see

Sincerity

Just one of many

The Expressions of Me….

Shown here as mere words

But there is something.

Something about,

The Expressions of Me

Look at me

To see as you will.

To focus on one's diversity.

Frown apon what you will.

Judgement is still yet,

Another's opinion.

Make your own.

Just another,

Still one yet,

To be..

The Expressions of Me.

The Heart Awakens

Faintly, the heart awakens from,
The sudden persistence the silence,
Questions the calming inferior on no
Control. A burden from silence,
Mooring to the root at hands end.
The branch extends until flowering.
Rhythmically, the sound continues
On still. A Heart from form.
A God sent image
For all, to adorn.

The light of God

Shall fall upon us.
With warmth
And guidance
We shall Never
Walk a lonely path
The light of God
Shall Fall upon you
Like Grace From his
Precious hands
The light From God
Shall always reside In You
As birth, As death.
The light of God
Is strongest
The light from God
Is always around you

The Struggler

Only the Struggler will survive.

The tough were beat, only to morn.

Can One man stand tall?

The match was a draw.

Who is powerful?

Who can be over powdered?

The Struggle, a match,

Which someone wins.

Then lose again upon another man's arrival.

Can One man stand tall.

Or is he easily over powered.

Can his match be made?

Will he stand tall?

Only the Struggler will survive.

He will beat his Match..

There comes a day
When all feels right,
But ends up to be all wrong.
The sacrifices that are made,
Resembles the belly of pain.
The power to continue
Brings much dismay.
For the weaker become.
Nothing, without say. I too must pray.
The sorrow to end,
The joy to return.
For the sorrow must,
Relinquish amongst the prey.
For I pray,
For tho who become lost,
Along the way.
As I to must pray.
For someone to be,
Rest a sure,
On this un- timely day.

This Day

Sorrow, for their own pity.
Shown reflected as a shadow.
Your own image, perhaps.
The essence of purity,
Dampens the torn
From healing perfectionless.
Merely, fragments of conjured
Speculation. Perhaps, none of the less.
Regardless, kwowing and changing
Are simple but complex definition.
A feasible, meddlesome, description.
Maybe, Human Error..

To cross The boundaries of lives Simplicities

A sure knowledgeable fact is easily detained.

A hardened Soul lacks The heart to live real.

The sought out endeavors mean nothing.

Only self appeal. A tired old remorseful soul.

Lacks remorse from the heart. A reminder to us all before

It's Too late to reconsider. As clear as the revolution of a new

day. A day Must be met to renew Your only life. A near death

experience you can say. But let's just, the rest of us, Pray For

the heart In this Tired old soul. To regain

The true purpose.

Of living one's Life.

Today, the day all creations,

Equally fight to survive.

Ones we never thought to exists.

Show their true form. Their might and will.

Too continue. They seek refuge no more.

Their tendencies ensure their survival.

For the rest, is surely a battle, many will morn.

Struggles from the battles they are torn.

Togetherness

Togetherness is foreverness

Jointly we are seamed.

With expressional love.

Attending and sharing.

To all that is certain.

Abiding to our destiny together.

We shall never walk alone.

Togetherness is absolutely a match.

All the way to Heaven.

Togetherness is willingness.

Togetherness is calmness.

Togetherness is coziness.

Togetherness is sensitiveness.

Togetherness is fo

Tomorrow is
Daydream Away

Only days away,

Which shall it be?

When tomorrow's desires,

Are so real to thee.

Tomorrow there is hope.

There is that certainty.

That there are dreams,

To be found.

Dreams to be made.

Seek and conquer,

As many as you can.

Tomorrow's Yesterday's

Seem long at first
But appear more memorable
Then Yesterdays thoughts.
Today's thoughts become
Yesterday's thoughts Today.
Today, soon to be yesterdays,
Reminder a faint glimpse of Today.
Compared to yesterday from long ago.
It seemed like by now.

What I do?

Too peer around,

Seems hopeless.

To scream out loud

Seems pointless.

Too the end of the battle,

Does it add up, to really matter?

Solitude is the Soul in comparison.

As we sought a meaningful purpose.

When our heart has no reasoning left to do.

When our mind shouts out everything it needs to do.

Fear from not knowing what are the heart/mind to do.

Staring, Alone Into the Vast World,

Sending out a message for help.

Through the eyes, until the hope

Is Lost.

From Your Eyes..

What Will
Become of Me?

What Will Become of Me?
When it's time,
All said and done.
How will I be remembered?
Who will Remember Me?

What will become, of my tired
Attempts to make it,
In this World?
The sacrifices that I
Lost along the way.
The Love and Joy
To always want to sing.
A positive rendering of
The Life Once Lived.

What Will Become of Me?
As the years become
Less of a memory.
Anniversaries, are a saddened,
Reminder of better days, long ago.

What Will become of
My tired attempts the positive rendering of
A Life, Once Lived.

Who Really Does?

Who really Does?
Care, appreciate all that you do?
Remember, what is dear to you.
Leads the example how to live
Your Life.
Paints the picture beforehand as the
Ornaments set to dry. Mom.
Who Really Does?
Concern themselves to conversate
A valuable, liable lesson.
The importance of having
Many desirable traits.
The heart for giving,
More then you have. Dad.
Who Really Does?
In the end,
There are only,
The two.

Why do I bother to try
When I feel
I want to die..
I feel all alone.
Is my Life really real..
For the one's whom
I wish would care.
You always treated me....
You nevered cared..
Why does my life
Even exsist at all..
It was never easy
To receive your love.
I tried I gave it my all..
I may have had my mistakes.
Lived with it all.
Now, I am alone
In a dire need.
Why should you care.
Why do I bother,
At all

You vs Me

Here we are,

A faint stare,

becomes the first,

too test your,

pure will, too outlast,

another, for a selfish purpose.

Solitary Gain, Victory over Defeat.

This moment above all others.

In your Heart, Preys within your mind.

Is it Revenge, or A Personal Gain.

You conjured this up, once before.

A Battle in which, "You have to Win."

As I place my Racing heart,

back into my chest. I am left a question.,

Is this just another test?

The anxiety, I can feel the rage,

burning to come out. I too, must

survive. Calm down...

Me vs You

If I am left too choose.
If there is me..
There will always,
Be You.
By J.D Van Anden

Your Life

Understand Yourself.

Feel for Yourself.

Set an Example for Yourself.

Know your Limitations

Take Control of Your Life

Explain yourself.

Be your own self.

Just understand, Your Life and You.

Could better Your own self.

It's Just. You,

Your Life..

Dear Mom,

If you could only read this.

In which you would already know.

That a Mother's Love is felt without none of us ever knowing. That your love is more abiding then hearing and touching you with the words Love You.. Love Mom… Expressing her enjoyment, is every Mother's Gift to us. A Mother's Love such as yours such as most is felt long after wards. When you always know deep down, your Motherly Love will always be there. As we progress, mature in our progression in Life. I may have never deeply, truly expressed my Love for you. For me myself personally I can just only imagine how deep your love for me was it will always be. Just by feeling others Mother's Love for their own loved one's. The picture is already there. A Mother's Love is endless..

Love Always,

Jeffrey Dean

Printed in the United States
by Baker & Taylor Publisher Services